A Child's Cry in the Shadow

Larvetricus Harris

©Copyright 2021 Larvetricus Harris

All rights reserved. This book is protected under the copyright laws of the United States of America.

ISBN-13: 978-1-954609-00-6

No portion of this book may be reproduced, distributed, or transmitted in any form, including photocopying, recording, or other electronic or mechanical methods, without the written permission of the publisher, except in the case of brief quotations embodied in reviews and certain other non-commercial uses permitted by copyright law. Permission granted on request.

For information regarding special discounts for bulk purchases, please contact:

LaBoo Publishing Enterprise at staff@laboopublishing.com
www.laboopublishing.com

All information is solely considered the viewpoint of the author.

Table of Contents

The Call 1

The Arrival 5

The Funeral 7

It Was Necessary 15

Mother 19

No More Home 21

First Prayer 25

Big Momma's House 29

"Centerville" 33

The Shadow 39

Ice Storm 43

Pregnant With a Promise 45

Ministry 47

My Choice 53

Chess vs. Spades 59

My Chess Move 63

Walking Out of the Shadow 65

About the Author 71

END NOTES

The Call

There had been several trips back-and-forth home. My childhood home was a place where I was raised and had never felt comfortable. My family and I stayed on the north side of Westtown, in the deep country called Centerville. Every time I went back to Centerville, it reminded me of my dreadful childhood experiences and the urgency I'd felt to leave back then. The earlier 12-hour drives and the nearly two-hour flights I'd done were necessary because my father was not in the best of health. I remembered it like yesterday; it was the Sunday before Memorial Day that my father called me around 1:43 a.m. in the morning to explain he had just been diagnosed with pancreatic cancer. Many people won't understand this, but that call was a sigh of relief. Why? Do not take this the wrong way. I loved my father, but sometimes I did not like him.

My father was a stout man, and even though he was pushing 60, he looked every bit of a young 50. He was a straight country boy who was mean, controlling, and very set in his ways. With only a high-school diploma he was a man that said little but demanded much. He knew everything about everything, even if that everything was not correct. In other words, he was set in his ways and no one could tell him any different. Being my father's oldest child, I had seen, heard, and experienced a lot. I had never known much about my father's upbringing, everything was kept a secret, but as you read on you will learn that my parents grew up as I did. They tried to raise me to the best of their ability as they too were just children when they conceived me.

You see, after his call about being diagnosed with cancer, every phone call thereafter was my father giving me the "just in case" information. To be honest, these conversations and these trips were overwhelming, and very disappointing. There were times he would fly me in for a day or two just to visit local business offices in Westtown to prepare for the day he would no longer grace this earth.

While I was at my house in Beachmount, I was not especially well for weeks. My father would call and talk for a little while, ask about my husband, my sons, and then hang up saying he loved me and we would talk later. Keep in mind, I did not grow up hearing from him or feeling he loved me. What was strange to me at that time was how he would continue the same conversations and questions, but in the closings, he started saying goodbye. My father never said goodbye. He always would say "talk to you later." It appeared he sensed the closing curtain was near.

Around 4:47 a.m. in the morning, my cell phone rang. It was my aunt. In a voice that sounded troubled, she said my father had died. Sadly, I never received a call from his wife. It was not until later I discovered her priority was her family, because she had just lost the love of her life. My aunt was even curious why she refused to call me, even though it would have only seemed right that she called his only living child. At the end of the call with my aunt she stated with concern, "LAKIA, GET HOME AS SOON AS YOU CAN!"

My husband and I immediately made the necessary arrangements to travel to Centerville to lay my father to rest. It was not until a day later, my dad's wife deemed it important to call me. Let us pause . . . and let me introduce her to you. Her name is Ginger. She is my father's third wife. The first was my mother, the second was Victoria, and then Ginger.

I am a very jovial individual. I get along with anyone. But I believe God used Ginger to test my character. She always wanted things her way, she tried her hardest to control everything and every conversation. She was the type of female that would say with one breath how much she loved God, and with that same breath cuss you out if she felt it was necessary. My first experience with her was when her and my father came to Seamount to visit my family and me. Every time my father visited, he requested to go shopping at this one store that had reasonable prices on clothes. So, on this particular day we went, everyone shopped and picked up the items of their choice. It was not until we got to the checkout line that she got so loud it became embarrassing. She went off because the line was not moving fast enough. I looked at my father and smirked, and with the most loving voice I could muster asked him, "You really married a woman like this?" I meant by the way she acted as this was not my father's taste in women. I knew then my father was facing a mid-life crisis!

After finding out my father has passed, my conversation with Ginger was not too pleasant, but I wanted to do my best in being there through this grieving process. I think she forgot I was his only living daughter, and I too was going through some tough mixed emotions. Even though she was his wife, only for 2.5 years, I was willing to devolve all information that could be a tremendous help in this strenuous time. As much as I did not want to deal with this, I had to garner all the strength I had and travel to a place I really did not like visiting—Centerville.

The Arrival

I stayed in close contact with my stepsister from my father's second marriage. This might seem very odd, but you must understand that after the death of her mother, Victoria, my father continued to play a role in her life. I could tell she was taking it hard. We discussed how weird it was that they had passed away at the same time of year: her mother passed days before my father in the same month, and my natural sister passed days after my father.

My family and I traveled for 12 hours to arrive in Centerville around noon. Once we were there, I was immediately put to work. From the last telephone call before hitting the road, I assumed everyone would pull together and make this the best homegoing service ever. But I found everyone bickering over nothing, and my father's wife asked me to write the obituary that the funeral home needed by two o'clock that afternoon. You had to be kidding me! I asked why this task was not given to his siblings. The response I got was so ridiculous: "I do not want them doing anything, they really do not love him." Right there, I knew this would be a roller coaster ride for the next seven days.

As I sat down to put pencil to paper, I realized I did not know the details I needed to make this a great story of my father's life. As his wife was somewhere puffing on sticks and drinking strong drink, I sat at the table and struggled to write something great. Finally, I got up from the table and walked next door to my aunt's house.

The Funeral

I only had two hours left until the service began. "Tis so sweet to trust in Jesus," I hummed to myself as I prepared for the day I never thought I would have to face. As the family laughed in the background reminiscing over their loved one, I sat listening to my heart thumping and racing with anxiety, I heard a familiar voice call my childhood name.

"Peaches, are you ready?"

I tried to move. I tried to get up. Again, I heard that voice.

"Peaches!"

My husband walked through the door of the bedroom I grew up in and shook me with his voice.

"Babe, they are calling you. Are you coming?"

"Sure," I responded.

As I slipped on my slippers, I grabbed my high-heeled shoes in one hand and tablet in the other. I stood up and took a deep breath and said to myself, "Okay, Jesus I trust you!" I could not believe that this was the day a request would be fulfilled, to preach my father's funeral.

As we walked towards the living room area, a thunderous sound came from the driveway. When we looked outside the window, we noticed a convoy of vehicles coming into the yard. It was Ginger's family driving into town for the funeral. They came in what looked like 15 cars, a motorcycle, and an armored tank. I could have sworn that I saw one of the family members in full camouflage with an assault rifle. I was uncertain what they were told about me, but it appeared they were coming in to stir up some trouble.

Although this seemed like this moment would be a great fight, I reminded myself that this day was not about me, but the people who would be at the church and other family members. I walked down the short hallway, but it seemed like it took forever to get to the living room. Before I could pick up the shoe I'd dropped, one of my children ran towards me and said, "Mommy, I got it."

"Thanks, babe," I responded. I turned the corner, put a look of strength on my face, and asked everyone in the room, "Are you guys ready?"

"Peaches!"

I turned to look at the voice that had been calling me for the last five minutes. It was my cousin, who was more like my auntie. A smile came across my face as I walked into the biggest hug. She tightened her grip and whispered in my ear, "We are here for you. Whatever you need, we got you."

I immediately had a flashback of my sister that had passed away five years ago. I remembered that day like yesterday, when no one seemed to care if I was there or if I needed anything. Everyone was just looking out for themselves. The same people who were dropping tears of losing a special person today, were that same ones that my little sister was calling me about asking for assistance in how to deal with the way they were treating her back then. A smirk crossed my face that my husband must have recognized. He placed his hands on my shoulders and gave me a look that suggested he knew what I was thinking. Instantly, I pushed the thoughts away and reminded myself again this moment was not about me. I had to remain strong for what was to come. I had to stand on the promises of God and deliver a word of hope to the people of God going through this tough situation.

As I walked outside, more people were standing and sitting on the deck laughing and sipping on juice that I knew was bitter and strong. I watched and listened to the family continuing to share stories of their journey with their loved one. I also heard sobs and Ginger was smoking on nature's natural herbs screaming she could not believe that this was really happening.

"God, why?" Ginger sobbed. "You left me here to deal with this all by myself. I can't do this, God! I loved him."

Everything in me wanted to shake her, but I reached my arm out to hug her and said with a low, conservative voice, "It is going to work out, you will be okay."

Her tears lightened, and her voice quivered with hurt as I continued to speak life to her. Ginger began to cope with the moment we were all faced with. As we continued to talk, I could tell hope was coming back to her. I took another deep breath and continued to whisper to myself, "This moment is not about me."

Everyone loaded up in the vehicles as the funeral director barked out orders.

Ginger yelled from across the yard like we were miles apart. "LaKia! Are you riding in the limo?" she asked.

"No," I responded.

"You and the siblings can ride in the limo. I am riding with my husband and children."

The cars were lined up in the planned order. As I looked at this precession, I thought how ridiculous this was. The three limos travelled less than a mile to the church. We could have walked to the church. I looked back at the house and could have sworn I saw a little girl run across the yard. I shook my head in disbelief, but I knew that I just seen me as a little girl grabbing my little sister by the hand and running towards my aunt's house to escape. This moment brought back so many memories.

Beep, beep. Beep, beep. Pulling into the parking lot of the church, a horn from a car woke me from this vision of the past. As I turned to look, someone was waving, trying to get my attention. Trying to stay focused on the task at hand, I slowly rolled down the window and stuck my head out to see what this person wanted. Before I could acknowledge the individual, I realized it was Beverly, a mentor I grew up with.

"Hey!" Beverly spoke.

"How are you doing?"

"I am doing fine," I responded.

Beverly spoke about how she felt part of the family, and how she was privileged to have known my sister and me. Standing beside the car, she continued to explain how she adored my little sister and was awed about how I had grown into a woman of strength and respect. Not really knowing what she was talking about, I was not interested in dealing with her at that moment. To prepare and gather my thoughts, I quoted C. S. Lewis, "Hardships often prepare ordinary people for an extraordinary destiny." If that is the case, there is something great in store for me thanks to this hurt! It was only by the grace of God that I was willing and able to do the things I had to in a season like this.

Car horns beeped and interrupted the quietness, which gave me the perfect opportunity to halt the conversation and focus back on the task at hand. As my husband opened my car door, I found relief in hearing the birds chirping and singing to themselves as though they knew this would be a good day. Regardless of the smell of rain, there was a sense of peace. There was a slight breeze swirling around the trees. You could hear frogs in the background as crickets sang their song. The smell of cows was inching closer and closer, as pigs oinked across the street. I was so glad I'd moved away from the country. Don't get me wrong, it was much calmer than the city, but the peacefulness I felt at this moment came with memories of pain and anguish.

At that moment, Ginger screamed, "Line up ya'll, we're about to go into the church. Come on, LaKia, you stand with me." She reached out to grab my hand as I slightly pulled back. Just then her son must have sensed something, as he came and stood beside her, as the waterworks sprang forth. The doors of the church flew open. People were already seated, and some stood around the wall of the sanctuary, as I wondered if anybody had thought about turning on the air conditioning. My God it was really hot!

As everyone passed the coffin, they admired how he looked. Suddenly, Ginger stumbled to the floor, shaking and stumbling for words. The ushers and others quickly gathered towards her to figure out what was going on. I envisioned myself taking the glass of water out of the usher's hand to throw on Ginger's face. You must understand, she is a person that is always seeking attention. She loved to make everything about her. Even though she was related to me by marriage, there was something that caused my skin to crawl when dealing with this selfish individual.

Maybe it was just me and this moment, but truly when do we become who God has truly called us to be? You can't say you truly love God but harbor so much disdain in your heart towards people. Even God states you cannot say you love Him, a God whom you've never seen, but hate people you see daily. It is impossible!

Yet, here she was rolling on the floor of the church, and every person helping her she had cursed out for various reasons. To let her wallow in her grief would seem like the thing to do, but NO, the God in me walks over to pull her up, throw my arms around her, and tell her it would be okay. "You are going to make it through this, I promise!" My uncle, my dad's oldest living brother, winked at me, to remind me of a previous conversation we'd had. He sat me down and said he was proud of how I carried myself the last couple of days. He said, "I have not said much, but I have been watching you and thank you for not making God look bad." I winked back at him, as a sign that I was doing my best to hold it together.

Friends and family continued to proceed inside the church to view the body. I walked over to my sons and nephews to make sure they were okay when my husband motioned to me to come towards him. I did not realize they had held the line to make sure I got all the time I wanted to view the body. As the organ played and my cousin sang, *In the Arms of Jesus*, the soloist sang, "When the storms of life are raging and the tempest falls on me, I'm safe. I'm so glad today that I got a hiding place, where the devil can't find me, where the storms of life can't get me . . ." I lifted my hands in worship. It was just too unreal to celebrate a man I did not respect in so many ways.

It Was Necessary

While the Hammond organ continued to hum, someone grabbed my arm and whispered in my ear, "They are waiting for you in the back." As I walked past my father's still body, I grabbed my husband's hand, squeezing it as though I was squeezing strength into me. I entered the Pastor's Study, the room where all the bishops, elders, and pastors were sitting, and once again all eyes were on me. I knew people were trying to figure me out as if trying to decipher my next move. As I sat in a chair waiting for others to arrive, I heard one of my favorite singers in my head, "I am who I am today, because God uses my mistakes. He's worked it for my good like no one else ever could. It was necessary!"

Once again, my mind wandered to the time when I was awakened from my sleep hearing a big bang. I jumped up and ran toward the sound to find Rene, my birth mother, in the corner of the living room screaming, "If you don't get help, he's going to kill me." Blood ran down her face and she was literally balled in the corner like a newborn baby, holding her head as he continued to release his rage on her, hitting her like an angry bear with no restraints. I felt hopeless. Why was my father doing this to my mother? I was too small to do anything. I pounded him as much as I could, as Rene yelled, "Call the police!" I kept pounding, trying to stop him, but nothing worked. Amid the screaming and yelling, I heard little feet come around the corner crying, "LaKia, do something!"

As I grabbed my little sister by the hand, I felt air underneath my feet as I was tossed about five feet away, like a loose ball. As much as I felt the pain, I picked myself up off the floor, grabbed the little hand, and took off running next door. As we reached the door, my superhero opened it up as though he had a telepathic mind. Our grandfather grabbed us both and wrapped his arms around us tight. "Go in there and lay down, I'll take care of you two."

Crying myself asleep while holding the little hand, I could not understand why in the world an eight-year-old had to face this. This made no sense to me! I tucked the little one underneath me, like a lion would protect her cub. I dried her tears and tried my best to comfort the five-year-old. WHY? I held my head, screaming inside. I could not let her see me cry, I had to be strong. I needed her to know everything would be okay in the morning, and we just needed to get through the night. Somehow, we had to get through this night.

As the sun peered through the window, I felt like my life was over. The door opened and a voice said, "Y'all come eat. Eat up now, ya'll going to need your strength."

Right then the side door opened, snapping me back into *now*, sitting here with the other ministers.

"LaKia," my cousin said, "you ready to robe up?"

I simply said, "Sure."

As she led me into the other room, away from the others, she encouraged me, as I was thinking about whether my life was necessary. Did a child have to go through that? As I took a deep breath, we headed back into the office with the others. As she opened the door, everyone stood up. I smiled as I saw my husband standing there and other familiar faces of strength. My bishop and the deacon from Seamount were there. The blessing was that they both flew to Centerville to support me and my husband during this time. Even though my spirit was heavy, my heart felt a little lighter seeing them. It is so true you can acquire much strength from others.

As we waited for the senior pastor to join us, the clergy in the room shared general ministry small talk. Some spoke of their years of pastoring. Some spoke of their years of marriage. A bishop asked my husband and I how long we had been dating. My husband looked bewildered. "Dating?" he asked. "Yes," the bishop responded. He expounded on the art of courting and relationship. He said marriage was an opportunity to continue to understand and date your spouse. We all thought that dating was a great tool to teach couples and a reminder to make sure that even though you're married, always remain friends by dating one another.

The senior pastor walked into his office where we were sitting, with Ginger following. In her squeaking tenor voice she said, "I wanted to come back here with y'all and see what y'all was talking about." Everyone looked at her and even though no one said anything to her, the pastor said, "Guys, let us get this service started." Each individual in the office grabbed the person's hand they were standing next to. The pastor led us in prayer for God to have His way in this service. Right before releasing hands, everyone looked at me and asked if I was okay. With so much on my mind, I simply responded with a half-smile, "I am fine." Out of respect, they also asked Ginger if she was okay. "God is good," she said loudly. Then for some reason, she used that as a door to explain how hard this was for her and all the pain she felt. Ten minutes later, she was still talking about the last days with my father and how she was the only one who really loved him. I just stood there, waiting patiently for her to get it out, but she continued until one of the bishops explained as nicely as he could that we needed to get into the sanctuary so the service could begin. At that moment, a staff member knocked on the door to motion for us to come into the sanctuary, as we were five minutes from the start of the homegoing service. Before we were ushered into the sanctuary, we received our specific assignments for the program. I whispered to myself, "LaKia, everything you have been through in your life was necessary for this very moment."

Mother

My mother was full of laughter and the most educated woman I've ever known. She walked with grace and was careful with her words, but ignorant about my father. I can remember her singing lullabies while preparing meals, teaching me how to read and spell my name. She would say, "LaKia, time for school! Today is M-O-N-D-A-Y, Monday." That was how she taught me the days of the week. She prepared every outfit for the school week on Sunday. I would go to my closet and look for Monday, and once I found it, I would yell back, "I found it. Today is Monday, M-O-N-D-A-Y." I loved learning, especially from my mother.

I was only in the first grade when my mother left home. She did everything for us to the best of her ability. When I came home from school, she always had my snack ready on the table. Play clothes would be on the bed and she went over my homework like a pro. As she assisted me with my homework, 30 minutes prior to my father coming home, she would cuddle my little sister and instruct us to always be strong no matter what. She would look at me with pain in her eyes and remind me to always take care of my sister. To make sure we stayed close. She told me I was a strong young lady and I would grow up to be something great if I obeyed Jehovah.

I thought to myself, "If I am so strong, why can't I help you fight my father?"

My father arrived home every day at 4 pm. We ate dinner together between 5:30pm–6pm. I thought they loved each other. We held hands as he prayed over the meal, "God is good, God is great, let us thank Him for this meal, amen." Questions were asked, laughter was exchanged. I would constantly think that maybe this would be the day I would sleep through the night. By 8 pm my sister and I took a bath and headed to bed. My mother would sit beside the bed and hum until we fell asleep.

And, like clockwork around 2am every morning, I would hear her scream. I knew this would happen, so I kept my shoes by my bed for quick access to get me and my sister out the house as quickly as I could. I moved quickly only to see my mother in the same corner she was always in as my father threw furniture, appliances, and words to hurt her. With the tears and blood streaming down her face, I thought to myself, "With all that you teach me, when will you tire of this?"

I was only eight when my mother walked out for good. That was the day I thought my mother would either die or my father would go to jail. I stood over my mother, and she grabbed my arm before my father threw me away from her, "LaKia, call the police, your father is going to kill me!" I picked myself off the wall and ran as fast as I could to get my grandfather next door. I banged on the door and he answered. Without me saying a word, he grabbed me by the hand as I led him to my house. After my grandfather finished with my father, I knew I would be an orphan. I was so scared!

No More Home

The night my father brutally beat my mother was the last night I saw Rene. That morning after my little sister and I ate breakfast, we walked back to our house. When we got to the front door, I peered through the front door window to see if it was safe to enter. I felt like I had just woken up from a bad dream. I walked through the door, my little sister waited on the porch, only to see the blood splattered everywhere. Nope, this was not a dream at all. "Think quick LaKia. How are you going to protect her?" I wondered.

She did not need to see this. I walked my little sister quickly to an aunt's house, who was married to one of my father's brothers, and asked if she could stay here while I cleaned the house. Do not get confused, we were raised in the country where your neighbors were your family. "Of course," she responded. She already knew of the situation.

You would have thought I had everything under control, as I walked back into a house that was no longer a home to me. Where did everyone go? I had seen Rene hit so many times. This was not the first time someone crying and being beaten had woken me. But, why did this time feel so different? I washed and wiped to the best of my ability. I picked furniture up and placed everything back in order as though nothing had happened. I swept the glass up off the kitchen floor. I wanted everything to be perfect. What did I do to make them act like this? I could fix this! I had to fix this! I needed to make this right!

The door opened, as I saw my mother walk through, just for a second, I felt the weight lift off my chest. "Wow! She is alive! Wait, she must have been next door the whole time," I thought. She just looked at me and continued to walk past me into her bedroom. I followed them as the door was closed in my face. What did I do? As I stood in front of the bedroom door, I heard her talking to my little sister, "Mommy is going to be okay." I jumped up as they opened the door, only to be pushed to the side and ignored once more. I thought again, "What did I do? Why is no one telling me it is going to be okay?"

With tears falling from my eyes, my little sister grabbed me while asking, "Where is she going?" I hugged her tight and proclaimed again to her it would be okay. That was the day I vowed I would never cry again; I had to be strong for this little one. I had to make sure she knew everything would be okay!

Ten weeks passed with no sign of Rene. My dad said nothing. My aunts and uncle acted as though nothing was strange. I wondered why something felt so different. I understood children could not say much about grown people's business, but had they ever thought, "You can keep me quiet, but you cannot stop me from thinking?" I was in the shadows of everything I saw and experienced, and no one cared. It had been 10 weeks since I had seen or heard from my mother. Feeling afraid of what came next, I laid across my parent's bed, as my father searched the Yellow Pages, calling random numbers trying to figure out where she could have disappeared to.

There was a knock on the door, and my father opened the door to my uncle. I was dismissed, but they clearly forgot I could hear. My uncle asked my father, "Have you found her? What are you going to do about the girls?" My father responded, "She has to be with her folks, but they are not telling me anything. I am going to need y'all assistance with the girls, and I hope they keep they mouth shut and don't go running telling everybody what is going on in my house!" If only they were paying attention, they would have seen I had never really left the room. I was like a shadow, and I had just moved out of sight. They were so preoccupied with trying to hide the truth, they forgot that there were two little girls that had just lost their mother. As they continued to talk, my fears turned into anger. I continued to listen while staring at my father thinking this was his fault.

First Prayer

No one was home. I squatted in a corner, not knowing what to do. The silence was unbearable. The darkness was scary. I had never been in this situation before. I was angry! If I needed help before, I had a mother or father to run to, but now I was alone. Thoughts of suicide were screaming at me to give in to it. I did not know what to do! Right when I thought I would give in to those thoughts I heard my grandmother's voice, "Jehovah, save my children!"

I did not know who this Jehovah was, but I mocked my grandmother, "Jehovah, save me!" Instantly, I remembered the words she taught us to say every time we went over her house, *"Hear, O Israel: The LORD our God, the LORD is One. And you shall love the LORD your God with all your heart and with all your soul and with all your strength. These words I am commanding you today are to be upon your hearts."* I didn't know what these words meant or if they would even help my situation! I was so confused! So, I just continued to talk to this Jehovah saying, "Please help me, help my mommy, help my daddy, help my sister. I am scared, and I do not know what to do."

I started laughing to myself at that point. Seriously, I was praying to someone I had never seen or touched, only a person

I had heard my grandmother speak about. Could this person really answer my prayers? Could this person really help my family through this mess? Just then, I heard a voice, "LaKia. LaKia, yes I love you! Just stand strong and I will see you through this."

By this time, I was rolling on the floor, laughing hard. What in the world was wrong with me? Now I was talking to myself. The day had been too surreal.

Feeling confused and lost, I went next door and asked my uncle's wife if she could take me to my grandmother's house when she went to the meeting that night. She agreed, and as we pulled up in front of my grandmother's house, my aunt looked at me and told me to wait one second. She gave me a Watchtower about "discovering your purpose". I looked at her with tears in my eyes, trying to figure out why in the world she would give me this. She had a very soft-spoken voice, but when she spoke it carried weight. She started explaining to me how special and important I was to Jehovah. She continued with how much He loved me and how He was calling me to be a witness for Him. I listened as she spoke. I was so confused why anyone would want me to testify for them.

"This is crazy!" I said. Of course, I did not quite put it that way, but let's just keep it unsoiled. The words must have hit a spot because my aunt popped my lips and told me, "Don't ever let me hear you speak like that! You are too beautiful to have language like that."

I dropped my head, trying to figure out why people refused to let me act like them. My uncle's wife did not say much about the situation, but she knew what was going on and what had happened that night. Soft, bitter tears rolled down my face as she told me that everything I had witnessed and would go through from this day forward was just training.

"What the hell?" I thought, but this time I kept my mouth closed. The words only sputtered in my head. How was that possible? How could I be someone Jehovah could use? Just as my grandmother came upstairs from the beauty shop in her basement, my aunt told me to always trust Jehovah even when I did not understand His plan.

The car door opened, and my grandmother shook her head towards my aunt. It was like they had this unspoken language that only they could understand. My grandmother gave me a hug and a kiss on my forehead and told me to go in the house. As I walked in her house, located directly upstairs from the shop, my grandmother and aunt continued to talk for a while.

Big Momma's House

I smelled the roast in the oven and a mixture of mothballs my great-aunt would spread throughout the house to keep the mice and snakes out. As I entered the house, a cousin ran to me and said, "I heard your dad beat the mess out of your mom last night." Really!

It felt like a fist just hit me in the chest. I just stared as he continued to describe to me the night I had just lived. All the while, I thought, "Jehovah, you really want me to trust You through this? This really hurts! Ahhh!"

Big-Momma's house was our safe house. A place we could come to chill and not worry about anything. Every other family member's house I was sent to for safety had similar issues. Even if it was another uncle, aunt, or cousin's house, it appeared their husbands were beating their wives as well. There was nowhere to escape. But being in my grandmother's house, my mom's mother, gave me so much peace. Just when I thought I could hide my pain, my hurt and my fear, it was jeered at right in front of me. I whispered to myself, "Jehovah, what is the real plan for my life?"

I loved this house! My grandmother had rooms for everyone that she loved. The house was always filled with either her children or us grandkids. If we did not sleep in the extra bedrooms, we would crawl in the bed with her, and she would put us to sleep reading the Bible as our bedtime stories.

My grandmother walked in, went straight to the kitchen, and fixed me a plate. Her food alone had you singing hymns for days it was so good! She asked me to come sit at the table with her while she took a lunch break from doing haircuts. I could see she was getting ready to talk to me about Jehovah, as she always had this certain look when she mentioned scripture. Keep in mind, I was only nine going on ten. What in the world could you tell a child to make them understand this crap?

The first thing she had me do was quote the scripture I had memorized: *"Hear, O Israel: The LORD our God, the LORD is One. And you shall love the LORD your God with all your heart and with all your soul and with all your strength. These words I am commanding you today are to be upon your hearts."*

"Good," she replied. "I am so proud of you."

Wait for it. Was that all she would say?

She continued, "Jehovah knows the plans He has for you; whatever you do, love Him with all your heart and strength." She looked into my eyes and said she did not know why my parents acted how they did. "Just remember Big-Momma will always love you and whatever you do, don't run from Jehovah, only run into His arms."

As I ate the plate of food that she prepared for me, I savored every bite. From the roast beef she simmered all night to the homemade mashed potatoes, six-layer macaroni and cheese, and chocolate pie, everything was on point! Oh, and the lemonade she sat outside in the heat all day was so refreshing! It felt as though I had not eaten in weeks, with everything that had gone on. Our grandmother rarely sat at the table to eat with us, not because she did not want to, but because she was always doing hair in her beauty shop. For the first time in a long time, my grandmother sat at the table with me, placing different sauces on my plate she had created to add flavor to her roast. The food was so good!

Finally, she got up to answer the phone. Whoever was on the other end, did not seem to make her happy. She hung up and explained my father was on his way to pick me up. I could feel my eyes watering as I silently pleaded with her to let me stay the night. I could see she was very exasperated from the conversation she must have had with my father. I did not care; I did not want to go back to that house.

"Eat up girl, he will be here any minute now!" she said.

I no longer had an appetite, but I stuffed the remaining food down with the little energy I had left, thinking to myself, "I am too young for this!"

"Centerville"

My childhood was interesting to say the least. For most of my childhood, I learned how to be a strong child, a strong older sister, a caregiver and to turn a blind eye. I knew my dad was not a monster per se. I just saw a man that only did what he knew to do when he was upset. He showed how powerful he was when he was punching and hitting my mother or manipulating and controlling others. When my father had a strong drink, I often watched him beat my mom.

Home was supposed to be the safest place for any individual. A place where you could escape from life and any hardships you may have faced throughout the day.

I was not a very attractive person. I felt like the runt from a litter of pups. In elementary school, I was bullied, and scared to ride the bus because someone always called you a "nigga" or a black "female dog." You must keep in mind I was raised down south, and I attended a predominantly white school. Quite honestly, the torment you endured from other classmates was not surprising. You knew exactly what they thought of you, if they thought anything of you at all. Racism was a learned behavior. I experienced it first-hand, and when you met their parents, you knew exactly why they treated you the way they did.

It was not until middle school, when enough was enough, I fought back. Something in me said, "I will not be like my mother." If I thought you would hit me, I would attack and try to paralyze you. I fought to kill or teach the lesson I would not be another female that a man or woman could beat. PERIOD! I said exactly what I thought, regardless of the consequences. Teachers attempted to reach out to my father, but he was always out of town. My uncle would come to the school on his behalf, but most of the time he was drunk and could only curse the teachers out for me. At the time, I loved it. He realized half the teachers I had, had also taught them in school. My grades were good, but I missed a lot of school to the point they held me back in seventh grade. Then, there was no such thing as "no child left behind." While my class went forward, I was stuck for another year in the same situation. I went nowhere fast! I was lost.

I became a little more serious in school and made it out of middle school, only to face the same situation in high school where people thought less of you because you were a person of color. But little did they know, I was growing up. My body finally caught up with my disproportionate big head. I played sports and lifted weights, continuing to make the point I was a force to be reckoned with. I would get kicked out of school and my father would plead with the principal to get me back in school, only to sit in "ISS" (in school suspension) for three to five days. The head principal of the school would appeal to me to use my mind instead of my fists. Every time a teacher called the office to have me corrected, the principal would show up. She would constantly ask me, "LaKia, what is wrong? Why do you continue to display this behavior?" One day she even took me to the guidance counselor's office hoping I would talk to them.

I thought, "Are you crazy? I wish I could tell you how scared I am to go home. I wish I could tell you that my dad stopped buying groceries for us to eat. I wish I could tell you that when I close my eyes to rest, I hear my mother screaming 'help' in my dreams. I wish I could tell you that when my father becomes angry, he will punch, kick, or throw me. I wish I could tell you that since my mother has left, my father has brought more women home than I can count. Can I really tell you that when my father gets drunk, he throws up and pees on himself and I am the one that is cleaning it up? Can I really tell you that my father uses drugs? Come on, really look at me. I wear the same clothes every day. I want to tell you I need help and do not understand why I have not seen nor talked to my mother in years. My father will kill me if I tell you what is going on in my household. But if I tell you what is really going on, I will get beaten up for telling family secrets."

How does a person seek help when you have been sworn to secrecy by your family? My environment constantly whispered, "You better not tell what goes on in this house, it is nobody's business, especially not the white man." My voice was minimized by what I had seen and knew. I needed help but could not raise my hand. People knew what was going on, but the same individuals that did the harm were the ones I should have been able to confide in.

Which brought me back to my point that Centerville was a rough experience. This city, this neighborhood, and this house were like sores to me. I often had seen horrific acts take place in this house. My father had often been out of control. Again, I asked myself, "Why do my little sister and I continually have to see this? Why in the world is my mom allowing this and won't fight back? Will anyone come and rescue us from this rampage?" Something needed to be done.

I looked back at my grandmother as I climbed in the back seat of my father's car. As I sat there waiting for him, I heard everything they said. My father had a rage in his eyes as he said sternly, "Tell her I just want to talk for a quick second." Not realizing what he was talking about, I saw my mother step out the house with her brother standing by her side. I sat in the car in shock. The whole time I was there, my mother was in the house? I put my hand on the window and whispered, "Momma." They stood and talked for what seemed to be hours, until my uncle told my father, "I think you should leave and cool off. This must be a nightmare!" My father jumped in the car, rolled down the window, while yelling to my mother, "Get in the car!" She shouted back, "No!" My dad pulled out while cursing under his breath.

It was still early as we traveled through the streets of Westtown home. You could smell the fresh manure as my father took the back roads home. I stared out of the window looking at the houses we passed by. They were spaced well apart, but it seemed shorter the way my father drove like a NASCAR racer. Flipping in and out of the curves on two wheels, my little body went back and forth. If it were not for the seatbelt, I probably would have fallen out the window. I really did not care; the only thing I could think about was being in the same house with my mother and she had said nothing to me. As we pulled into the driveway, my dad's dad was sitting on the porch. I jumped out the car and into my grandfather's arms. I loved that man; he made living in the country fun.

My house was in the middle of my uncle's and aunt's house on both sides; as a matter of fact the only people who stayed near us were my father's nosey family. You could do nothing without them knowing. Every chance my father had, he would tell us how he built the house when he was 21 years of age with no help. We had a decent three-bedroom home and plenty of land to play outside. Woods filled with animals, ponds, and trees surrounded the house.

My grandfather was a pure country man that had worked all his life. He was a farmer that knew how to grow a seed into vegetables or fruits. As my grandfather approached the car, he told me to run on over there to my aunt's house, my dad's oldest sister, because they had something for me. My aunt came across the field with a cup of buttermilk and the homemade biscuits my grandfather had made just for me. As my grandfather sat back on the porch, he put me in his lap as I ate what he had prepared for me. I was not really that hungry, but my grandfather's biscuits were so buttery, they melted in your mouth.

While sitting there, my aunt went into the house to speak to my father concerning the craziness that went on last night. Out of nowhere, my grandfather said, "I think you should come stay with me and your aunt for a while." I was so confused. Did my father not want me now either? I felt like giving up. Why did someone so young have to go through this? Why did they even have me? I replied, "Whatever you all want me to do." I felt like the shadow cast over my life had just gotten darker.

The Shadow

I lay on my aunt's floor while she was on the couch speaking to my grandfather. He must have thought I was asleep.

"Something is wrong with him, Daddy."

"I told y'all he had problems." My grandfather reached for me and picked me up as he said, "Y'all are crazy!" As he laid my head on his shoulder he said, *"He that dwells in the secret place of the most High shall abide under the shadow of the Almighty."*

What? Not this again. Why did everyone quote scriptures to me and over me?

He continued as he personalized it, *"I will say of the LORD, He is LaKia's refuge and fortress: my God; in You she will learn to trust. Deliver Kia from the snare of the fowler, and from the noisome pestilence. Cover her with Your feathers, and under Your wings shall she trust: His truth shall be thy shield and buckler. She will not be afraid of the terror by night; nor of the arrow that flies by day; Nor of the pestilence that walketh in darkness; nor of the destruction that wastes at noonday. A thousand shall fall at thy side, and ten thousand at thy right hand; but it shall not come nigh thee."*

It was a long scripture. Geesh, Granddad!

He set me on his bed, smirking at me. "I know you are not sleep."

I yawned but could not help but smile back at him. I looked up at my grandfather as he spoke.

"Remember when I took you to the watermelon patch?" Not waiting for an answer, he continued to explain that before the watermelon grew, he had to break up the fallow land. "I had to take the land given me that was unfit to plant anything. You must keep in mind, I worked as a slave man. Sometimes I did not get money as a payment, but people offered land as payment instead. They gave me land in the middle of nowhere, land that they thought was unfit to use. For years, the owners could get nothing to grow. In that era, African American men were considered useless individuals that did not deserve the best of anything. Not only did other cultures consider me useless, I also faced in-house rejection by my own peers, family, and people that looked just like me. It is one thing to be rejected by others, but it is a deeper pain when your own kind want nothing to do with you."

"What does this have to do with me? I am so confused!" I said.

My grandfather had a strong voice, and he responded with the bass in his voice and continued to tell his story. "Sweetheart, the land they gave me was rough and useless. And, just like you, I questioned life and everything God had planned for me. But I worked harder and despite what people thought of me I learned how to turn trash into treasure with the sweat of my hands. The land was rough and full of bushes, trees, sticks, and trash. At first, I struggled, I constantly argued and rebelled against those who gave me the land. I thought I was what people said I was. I was trash just like this land."

Wow, I thought, my grandfather felt just like me—trash.

"I watched the ones I worked for day and night, I took the little money I had and invested in a backhoe and other equipment I needed. I plowed the stubborn ground that did not want to yield any fruit. Day and night I plowed, raked, and plowed more. Finally, I saw one green leaf sprout from the ground, and that is when I knew it was worth it. Something told me to plant the seeds deeper than you were supposed to. So, I went deeper and before you know it, I had a field full of watermelon. I cried so hard that day, because I had done what no one could do."

"What does this have to do with me?"

My grandfather explained I must dig deeper in my faith and depend solely on God, as my life would depend on it. He taught me how to push past my pain and be who God would have me to be. He taught me how to stand and work hard no matter what people said or thought.

I had seen my father control my mother physically numerous times. She was thrown in a corner bellowing for her life. When asked if she needed help, my father was her ventriloquist, and she would respond no. My grandfather explained how I had to learn not to say much. He operated in the shadows to survive in a world filled with hatred. I told him, "Granddaddy, I feel like I am stuck in a shadow too and I want out." I thought my grandfather would give me step-by-step instructions about how to be a big voice and walk out of the shadow. Instead he said, "Stay there." What! Really! Why? "You'll understand it better as you get older," he finished. It was the same line every adult loves to tell a child. Just great!

Ice Storm

My family was religious on both sides. Depending on whose house you were over, they were a Jehovah's Witness, Muslim, Catholic, Baptist, or just a straight sinner. Everybody believed in a higher power. Regardless of what they taught or what I experienced, I knew I was called to be a preacher.

We had been out of school for about a week, and I decided to read some Bible stories I had heard others talk about. I remember it just like yesterday; in 1989, one of the greatest ice storms hit. I was 11 years of age and chilling at my aunt's house, when I felt pressed to read the entire book of Revelation. Everybody was gathered at her house because she had a wood stove downstairs. And, while there was no electricity, we ate well! That was the week I learned how to trap rabbit, kill it, strip it, and prepare it for a meal. There is nothing like some good ol' rabbit cooked on top of a wood stove, smothered in gravy, and with a sidekick of homemade biscuits. As I read, everyone slept, but it was like a voice was telling me to always preach the good news. The house was silent. How in the world did you get something like that out of reading Revelation? This was strange to me! I searched for someone to help, but my family was still sleeping off the strong juice they consumed the night before. I was scared, but not scared. I knew Jehovah was speaking directly to me through the scriptures. So, I got up and got dressed. I was ready to embrace the cold. I had no idea what I was thinking, but I had to do it. I grabbed my aunt's choir robe, stood on her front porch and quoted what I heard my great uncles and grandfather say when it was their turn to pray as deacons in the family church up the street.

"I stand here coming before you today, head bowed, and body bent. Lord, I thank you that last night my bed did not become my cooling board. And, oooh, God, I just want to take a minute to tell ya, thank you! Thank you, Jesus, oooh, thank you, Lord. Thank you that you kept me when I did not know how to keep myself. And, I thank you that you never left me, and you've been with me every step of the way. Lord, if nobody else brought a thank you today, I just want to tell you I am much obliged, Lord . . . Lord, touch the sick and heal the shut-in."

By that time, something in me snapped. I slid back and forth on the ice, screaming and shouting "thank you, Jesus." I felt a release I had never felt before. I went back to praying the prayer the ol' deacons prayed, but couldn't because I was at the point in the prayer you could not understand what they were saying. So, I switched over and prayed what I heard an aunt and my grandmother prayed: *"Jehovah, you are Lord. And, Father I just want to thank you that someday if I continue to live to the best of my ability that I will get to see paradise."* Something in me was stirring, so I laid hands on our dog Bellow. If only I could have read his mind. I did not know I had a crowd gathered around the windows in the house until someone shouted, "She outside running around in the yard preaching to the ice and laying hands on Bellow."

Pregnant With a Promise

It was at that moment I knew God had a plan for me. I remember yelling in the airwaves, "You have just now been impregnated with a promise." The only thing my family heard was pregnant, and boy did they run outside in a hurry. I just looked at them, as I was now preaching to them they were "pregnant with a promise" and God would do something special just for them. As one or two cussed me out for dragging them out there in the cold, I laid hands on them. I had no idea what I was doing, but I knew I felt the power of God. I told them there was a promise in each of them, and God just told me I was pregnant with a promise. Of course, I was the talk of the day. I knew eventually the story would be unfolded.

I stood there pointing at this big tree, and spoke directly to it. Little did I know I was preaching to myself: "God said he knows exactly what you are facing right now, and as your mid-wife I want to let you know that you are in your last trimester. Your water is about to break! God is getting ready to bring forth that promise, that blessing that you thought was forgotten." I looked at the next tree and explained that just as a mother is pregnant and expecting, she too must wait until the baby is developed enough to come into this world. About that time, everybody sent my father out the house to get me; they wanted him to get me in the house before I "caught a cold in my buttocks." But it was not until tears fell from my eyelids they knew I was not playing. I knew then there were some things in me being worked out and developed. I told myself to stop beating myself up. And though I felt like I was all alone in this world, God would teach me how to stand strong.

Ministry

After that ice storm, I was excited to tell people my experience. I wanted everyone to know that I had been called to preach. I stood boldly, without blinking my eye, and explained that God would use me. God told me I was "pregnant with a promise!" I had a word for people. Just like the book of Revelation, I told my family, friends, and everyone that would listen to repent for the Kingdom of God was near! Little did I know, the more excited I became, my surroundings thought different. My family echoed the voice as one choir, "You are too young to tell me to stop doing what I am doing! How can you preach? Do you realize you are a woman? I can't let you in my pulpit. If you want to remain in this church, don't tell anyone you have been called to preach. Wow, I never thought you would come my way."

I remembered what my grandfather told me; it was one thing to be rejected by strangers, but it was another type of hurt when the people who looked like you also rejected you. How could you stand on God's word when everyone around did not believe it was God? I felt like I had just been smacked in the face. I'd finally felt a love that I'd never known before. I felt complete, but everyone that could push me to reach my potential were the very ones telling me I was wrong. According to some pastors, God would never tell a woman to preach the word. They said, "Your job is to get married and have kids." I was the child that always must stand in someone's shadow. Would I ever have my own voice?

I gave my voice up and did whatever I saw my cousins do. I was only allowed to hang around certain people. In all my father's craziness, he did not allow us to spend the night over anyone's home he did not know. I remember asking my father years later about this. It was too funny how he said with a straight face, "Because I did not want you telling my business, sometimes you talk too damn much."

Even though I was a child, something kept me from going wild. We hung out late, we smoked weed, and drank strong wine. We stole money and threw birthday parties on someone else's dime. I was affiliated with gangs, fought, and stole cars. From the age of 11 to 14, I was in my own world. I figured I'd create my own voice, so people would know I was serious about what I believed. I was like the pig my grandfather kept on his farm; every time it had an opportunity, it would break loose and run wild. I was running wild! Well, that is what I thought, as God still had his hand on me. The farther I ran away from God, the closer he would pull me to him. I was still reading His word, I was still praying, and going to church. I was looking for something but did not know what that was or how to find it. I tried things that I knew would disqualify me being loved by God. I remember when I was hanging with an older cousin in the Heights. I did things I saw them do, but everyone told me to sit on the couch and watch TV. These folks really did not care, but for some strange reason, they would not allow me to hang out too late unless I was with them. I could not even go outside by myself. They would throw house parties, but I would have to go into a room and just sit there.

* * * * * * *

I grew up very fast after my mother left home. I experienced freedom at a very young age. Even though I was free to explore, I could not. Something had a hold of me and would not allow me to run totally crazy. When I was not with my Big-Momma, I was with my aunt, and she took me to church. I ushered, sang in the choir, and taught Sunday School for the youth; I was there when the doors opened and most of the time picking up the last piece of paper before the lights went out.

I was never a disrespectful youngin' for some strange reason. It was like there was an invisible line drawn within me that pulled me back in every time I got close to something. Let me reiterate that everything I did was with my family. My lineage on both sides taught me how to drink, smoke, lie, steal, fight, and deceive. I knew how to get what I wanted, when I wanted it, and it did not matter who got hurt in the process. The more I drew closer to that invisible line, I pushed it further out to do more things that caused self-destruction.

I can remember the call like it was yesterday. The phone rang, and it was one of my cousins telling me we had been caught. We had withdrawn money from an account that did not belong to us. My cousin explained the bank had pictures of me and knew exactly who I was. I was scared out of my life, yet relieved. I had to tell my aunt and boy did she let me have it! And, though she cussed me out like it was nobody's business, she protected me from my father. She explained very thoroughly that if my father were to find out, he would kill me because it would embarrass him, not because he really cared. I had to face that person and apologize, along with explaining how I would pay the money back. That was the first time I had to face a situation I got myself into. I could have gone to prison for 25 years, but I was grateful the charges were dropped.

Along with repaying the money back, I had to attend a revival with my cousins. It was an outside tent revival, right in the middle of the projects we hung out at. I walked into that tent thinking, "Let us just get this over with." I sat in the front row, standing, sitting, yelling, and clapping when everyone else did. I was mocking what I seen to get through this torture as quickly as possible. I loved God and respected the church, but it was hot as Hades outside and I was ready to go! Five hours later, the service finally seemed to be ending. Right before the man of God was getting ready to close out, he said, "Come here, daughter." I looked around for his daughter, wishing whoever she was would hurry up. He repeated himself, "Come here, daughter." As I continued to look around, I noticed everyone was looking at me. If they had read my mind, they probably would have stopped staring. I turned towards the preacher and noticed he was looking right at me. "Come here, daughter!" There was so much authority in his voice that my legs just walked towards him with no hesitation. I stood there, while he starred at me, grunting, and saying, "Yeah, Lord." I wondered how many times he was going to say, "Yeah, Lord?"

I became a little frustrated, so I looked at my watch and noticed it was 10:30 pm. We had got here at 5:30 pm. I was so tired! He looked at me again after circling me for the third time. Then suddenly, as he put his hand on my shoulder, he called for some older ladies to stand with me. I thought the old people were getting ready to jump me. He spoke, "Daughter, do not be afraid or concerned, God is confirming what you already know." I was puzzled. I knew what God had spoken to me, but what did this man know? Again, he opened his mouth, "God is birthing something in you . . ." Uh oh, I felt a little woozy. I felt tears swelling in my eyelids. He continued, "Daughter, you are pregnant with a promise, and God is calling you forth in ministry . . ." What do you mean, calling me forth in ministry? If he was talking about preaching, everybody I knew had told me a woman could not preach. As I was saying this to myself, the man of God said, "Yes, you are going to preach. People are going to come against what you know God has spoken to you, but, daughter, I need you to learn to listen to the voice of God, and when He speaks to you, lean on His words and not on the doubts of others." He continued to explain to me the things I was struggling with eternally. As quick as I asked in my head, he answered. I knew for sure when I left that tent, God was going to use me. Right before I hit the ground, I heard him say, "Turn your pain into ministry."

As the older ladies pulled me off the dirty ground, I noticed others were still praying for me. They were asking God things for me on my behalf. I was amazed people that did not know me were praying for me. Not only were they praying for me, they were speaking in a funny language that I had never heard before. I dusted myself off and knew something was different about me. Leaving that tent, I knew if I wanted to fulfill God's promise I had to make some major changes.

That week, I changed how I looked at life. From that point, I learned to just believe God's word, no matter what others said, and boy, did I get challenged!

My Choice

I was not the same person I was before that tent revival, but I was far from perfect. I still had to learn how to say no and stand on what I knew to be true. For the very first time in my life, I got ready to become part of a church I was not drafted into, but one I chose for myself. I felt free and liberated, content. I had already been baptized once, but when joining this church, I was told that I must be baptized in Jesus' name. I was willing to do anything that would bring me closer to God. So, I agreed to be baptized again. I guess the first baptism did not work.

Now the funny part is, when I chose a church for myself, the family went into action immediately. They had the nerve to call a family meeting to discuss how they thought it was not right for me to be a part of this church. Man, where was this family meeting when my father was beating my mother, and my sister and I had nowhere to go? Where was this family meeting when the abuse turned to me? I was livid! Even my father spoke, "Either stop going to that church or I'll take your car!" he shouted. I simply laid the keys down on the table next to him and said, "Okay, I'll walk."

It may be hard to believe, but at age 14 I just wanted to see God for myself. Not only was I baptized again, but I was taught that for me to see God, I had to speak in tongues. What in the world had I got myself into? Yet I did not care; if it bought me closer to God, I was willing to do whatever it took. So, I went to the church every night and laid at the altar saying Jesus so many times until I started speaking in that unknown language. Even though it took weeks, I was finally filled with what they say was the Holy Ghost. After weeks of doing that, I was told that I would have to stop wearing pants and shorts! I was a ballplayer; I loved playing sports. I was told that women were to only wear skirts and dresses, and anything other than that would send you to hell. Not only could you not wear pants or anything of that nature, but you were not to wear jewelry, make-up, your skirts had to be below your knees, and you could not show any part of your feet or toes—everything had to be covered to be considered a modest woman. Movies, skating, bowling, concerts, prom, and games were carnal and out of God's will. You may be wondering why I stayed? Keep in mind, anything that I thought or was told would bring me closer to God, I would do, even if it seemed crazy!

My family said I was allowing the Jesus people to brainwash me. They never took into consideration that I had fallen in love with the people of God, them folk. My family forgot that the only thing I'd seen from them were my father hitting my mother, the drinking and acting crazy with each other, and the accusations where they all blamed each other for something. I wanted a way out from an atmosphere that produced hatred. And if the Jesus freaks treated me respectfully, I would do anything. I just wanted a little peace in my life.

I loved my family dearly; they were fun to be around when they were not acting like a group of mafia kings. If they weren't arguing and fighting about who was buying what, they would fight over the land my grandfather had left. It was always something! But these people I had just met invited me into their homes and I ate dinner with their families. I traveled with them and got to know other young people doing and acting the same way I was. I had always ushered and taught Sunday School at the church I was raised in, but my new spiritual family understood that I had a calling on my life, and they taught me everything I needed to know when it came to church. I might have bitten off more than I could chew, but I was a sponge, and I soaked up everything. They mentored, led, guided, and motivated me about how I should carry myself in the ministry. Everything seemed great!

I grew close to the first lady of the church; she was cool. She treated me like her daughter, and I even called her mom. I felt like a child. I felt like God was redeeming the years I had lost. I felt like I was back on track to having a real childhood, without having to worry about any and everything. The tomboy in me was being transformed. Mrs. Freda, the woman I called mom, taught me how to walk in heels and dress like a lady. She taught me how to walk in a room without saying anything and demand respect. I learned through her that a woman could have a voice, preach, lead, and still be a lady.

Not only was I learning how a lady should act, but I also learned true servanthood. I was at every prayer service and fasted when told I needed to fast. I attended every revival. I sang in the choir, led the testimony service, stood in the office as a junior deacon, evangelized, played instruments when no one else would show up, and led the youth and single's group when needed. I was so dedicated that they gave me keys to the front doors. I was willing to do whatever it took to serve God and His people. I even wore the hat of a janitor. I hung wallpaper, painted, decorated, and nailed nails where needed. I was the first to show up and one of the last to leave. I can honestly say, I know how to serve. I learned to give my all. I learned how, and as my grandfather instructed me, to give one hundred percent regardless of what anyone else said or did.

I was part of a church that reminded me of my experience at the tent revival. I was being used and preached my first sermon at 18 years old. My father was right there, celebrating with me, along with family members that could not believe I was going to preach. A year later, my Spiritual Father pulled me into his office and explained why he had not asked me to preach since my first sermon. He explained he wanted me to study and continue to seek God. But he also stated God would use me, and told me to stay humble. He said I should never allow myself to think more highly of myself, and to always show mercy to others.

Being with this ministry allowed me to be a part of an organization. I could travel and hang with other young people my age that worked in ministry just like me. I learned to operate in the five-fold ministry; a term used to define the church's leadership ministry. I wanted everything that God had for me!

As years went by, I felt free, but something was missing. Now that I could stand on my own, meaning I had now graduated from high school, I was living with my spiritual parents and seeing family from a different view. They were not perfect at all, but they did their best to love each other so much. We were in church almost every day of the week. I saw the affects that the "church" could have on your family. I saw members pay their tithes but let their children sit in the dark and wonder where their next meal would come from. I saw how leaders gave their time to others but did not show any interest in their own children at home. I often wondered where the balance was between the church and your home. Not only that, but I wondered if there was more to this than preaching, shouting, and speaking in tongues. I wanted more but did not know exactly what I wanted. I loved these people, but I wanted more from God. I was in a church that offered me the world, but I felt empty.

I am not perfect, but I made a vow to God, I would do my best, and give my all. It was a commitment. The crazy part of that whole vow was keeping my promise even when others were doing less. I realized the more I gave, the less others gave. People pimped me for my abilities. I knew I was being used, but I wanted God more. With all that I was doing, I was in a dry place. The older I got, the more I saw. I began to even see the politics in church, the business side of things. It goes to show you that your title and working in a church will not bring you closer to God. I was tired of watching individuals portray who they proclaimed they were in God. I wanted less of church and more of God.

Chess vs. Spades

I went to a mentor for guidance about what I felt. I told her I wanted more of God and less church. She acted like I was about to kill someone. Looking back, I realized I was trying to get guidance from a person who associated church with God. Speaking to them concerning how I felt was like telling them they did not love God. I learned from that conversation it was best to fast and pray until you heard from God. So, my prayer was, "God what is next?" Keep in mind, friend, you cannot be serious and ask a question like that and think God won't change your circumstances. It was the same question I asked when I was a child facing hatred, abuse, and pain. I thought of conversations my aunts, Big-Momma, and grandfather had with me. They reminded me how much God would direct your path. How Jehovah would always protect you from unseen dangers. It reminded me I was full of promise, so I knew the answer was already within me.

I was never a chess player, and took no interest in it as I thought it was quite boring. But I knew about spades! I learned from the best: my father and my family. Not knowing how to play spades in my family was like a cow not being able to produce milk. It was mandatory! In spades, you got your hand, talked it over with your partner and you bid, hoping everything played out like you planned. In the same way, you bid on decisions in life and prayed that everything worked out. But I learned the hard way that life would be more effective if you learned how to play it like chess. Chess is a game built from strategy; to succeed from the very first move, you must plan the end. It is a game of patience that requires you to make sacrifices of one of your pawns or a knight to advance further in the game.

One night I spoke to a good friend, Shay, that I met through my baby sister. She invited me to her church. It was a Thursday night and I had no plans, so I went. When I walked into this church, I saw people walking around in a circle, reading what was on the wall, then demonstrating what they had read. I realized later that they were in a series on prayer. It was just what I needed! I was in a dry place wanting less church and more God, and it was better for me to ask God for guidance than my elders. They reminded me that they thought I did not know how to hear from God myself, just like my family when they thought I was crazy because I knew God was calling me to preach His gospel.

I did not hop from church to church for fun, but I truly believed God was trying to get my attention. I began to visit that church on the off nights I was not doing anything at my church. I felt like God was setting me up for something greater. I knew He'd led me to that place of worship on that particular Thursday night when they were teaching on prayer. So, I continued to visit and after a while I joined. When I made that move, all hell broke out in my life when I had to deal with others outside that church and my family. Once again, my family decided to call a family meeting. My father, who appointed himself my preaching manger, had a fit when

I told him I would not be preaching for a while! If anything, I learned that when you follow God, you will lose friends and gain enemies.

As soon as I joined this church, the pastor explained I would not be used to preach like that in his church. I just wanted more of God and I had learned how to be patient to see exactly what God would do. I taught classes instead, did home bible studies, and worked with the young people at this church. He told me in a very soft spiritual way, using scripture, that he did not want me to assert myself like I was a preacher and to always remember that he was the pastor of this church. I played it cool, because just like in spades you never showed your hand; in other words, always smile and never show how displeased you are when people try to check you in a spiritual way when it really was control. I was not an ignorant young lady, and had a father who was controlling. I knew firsthand how you could orchestrate your words to get what you wanted.

I had seen this outside the church and now inside the church. Individuals from the other church, along with some family members, asked for the things back they had given me. My dad took the car he had given me, the first lady from my previous church collected the suits and clothes she had given, and some family members spread lies against me. I guess they felt they needed to take back everything that they had let me have, because I decided to go in another direction. I was confused and hurt, but God was teaching me how to solely depend on Him. Once again, I just wanted more of God.

I felt like that child again walking in the shadow of others. As I began to grow in ministry at Front Street Apostolic

Church, they pit Shay and I against each other. She was my best friend, but every meeting that the pastor had with me he tried to put us in competition with each other. Along with that, he knew my former pastor and wife, and whatever beef they had against each other they took it out on me. My previous pastor's wife constantly reminded me I should not be at that church and my new pastor told me I should leave the past behind and not continue to talk to them. He told me to be careful how I entertained their conversation, because they were jealous of him and his church. The constant bickering was working my nerves—I just wanted God!

I am so thankful that I did not become the woman of God they wanted me to be; instead I became the woman God wanted me to be. While I was always betting with my life like I was playing spades, God was playing chess. He was strategically making moves for my future behind the scenes, He was showing me how to walk out of the shadow to become my own person.

My Chess Move

I loved the new church, and it was fun. We had some good crazy times, but I knew from the beginning I was only there for a season and this would not be my destination for life. I've never forgotten the calling on my life to preach. I never gave up on that, but I knew there was something there that I needed. I communicated that to the pastor when I first joined, and we had our one-on-one meeting on expectations of the position I would occupy at the church. I served that ministry for about six years. I remember the day Shay took me to the Pastor's house so I could explain to him I was resigning and moving north. I was at a crossroads. My Spiritual Father had just passed away and my Spiritual Mother was hurting trying to pastor a church she did not want. I told her I could come and assist her until she got through the grieving season and she agreed. Not only that, I wanted to be closer to my little sister. She was all grown up with kids of her own; but word was getting back to me that she was going through something like our mother had done. I did not want her to experience that and something had to give.

It was a hard decision! It appeared I was walking away from the young people I was mentoring and the children in the day-care that Shay and I owned. I was not in a hurry to leave, and

I refused to leave the wrong way. But after the conversation I had with the pastor, I knew I would not be there much longer. The pastor told me not to tell anyone I was leaving, not even my group leader. He said he did not want them thinking it was okay to walk out of the will of God. What do you mean walk out of the will of God simply because I was leaving your church to continue in ministry at another church? You had to be kidding!

Things got rough! My group leader called and asked if he could meet with me. When we met, he asked me why I had not told him I was leaving. I twisted my head at him like a confused puppy and explained it was because the pastor asked me not to. It turns out the pastor had told certain individuals and members of the church I was leaving because I had fallen from the grace of God. I continued to talk to my group leader for a long time after church was over, and I laid out the whole situation. I was not sure anyone else knew the truth, but I had learned at a young age never to chase a lie. My time there had ended, and I knew God was shifting me out quicker than I had planned.

Walking Out of the Shadow

As I lay on the floor, I pounded it with all my might. Tears flowed down my face like a river overflowing from a reservoir. The pain would not stop. I felt as though I was vomiting pain and a bunch of heartache. My head felt it would burst into a million pieces. So many memories flooded my thoughts like reruns on a television. I felt each punch I had seen my father deliver to my mother. I felt every lie told about me. I felt every betrayal from the church. At this very moment, it seemed like I was being forced to face my child self. Why now? Why was this 42-year-old now realizing I had never really confronted some situations, but just remained silent as if afraid of what someone might say, think, or do to me? Why had I stood in the background all those years? Why were all these feelings coming to a head? Why did it appear God was pushing me to deal with the little girl inside?

While feeling this unknown pain, my mind drifted back to when my family and I were on our way to a vacation when my father called. If I know who the person is when they call me, I will always answer the phone by saying their name to be intentional on purpose.

"Hey, Daddy," I answered, "what's up?" He told me he was okay, but he had just left the doctor's office and found out that the cancer had metastasized to other organs in his body. After a quick conversations with my husband, we changed our plans and drove the 12 hours to Centerville. My husband felt it was imperative to visit, and the boys should see their grandfather one last time. Something in the air told us this was it.

When we arrived at my father's house, he was relaxing in his chair. When my husband and I walked in he smiled, but when he saw my boys, his smile widened. Forgetting he was weak, my youngest jumped on him screaming, "Granddaddy, I love you." You could see the pain in his face, but the smile remand as he responded, "I love you too." He looked like the little skinny bigheaded boy that my aunt would show me in the pictures of their childhood.

My father was probably showing off, or trying to make me think he was one hundred percent, so he jumped up and said, "Let us take a ride, I want to share some things with you." After much convincing, I talked him into delaying that ride until the next day. The next morning, he decided he wanted to drive. After hitting the first curve, I knew I was in for a treat and had made a major mistake letting him sit behind the wheel. Somehow, I needed to get him from behind the wheel and drive myself as he was scaring the living daylights out of me. As we continued our journey, the most memorable stop was at the gravesite located directly behind the church I grew up in. We walked around and cleared weeds from some family graves. Then he looked at me and said, "Follow me," and took me to the spot where he wanted to be buried. I took note and said, "Dad, first thing Monday morning you need to get with the deacons of the church to make sure that spot is available." My father gave detailed explanation about the steps he wanted me to take after he passed. He reminded me I was to deliver his eulogy; I smirked and said he should let his wife know. He said sternly, "What did I say?" I answered, "Yes, sir."

I was confused. Why would my father want me to preach his funeral? As he and my husband joked about something, he noticed my facial expression. He said, "You are stronger than you think and your dad will not be around much longer. I need you to come out the shadows and just live." I only had one full day to spend with him and he used every single minute of it. He gave me instructions about what to do and a lot of instructions about what not to do. In his own little way, he gathered things together to the best of his ability, because after his passing I was given handwritten instructions on what accounts to take care of immediately versus the ones that had nothing to do with me.

Before we left and headed back to Seamount, I asked him, "If I never see you again, what is it you want me to remember?" He looked at me and told me to look at a certain tree. I looked at that tree as he reminisced about how me and my cousins used to shoot ball on that tree. He said, "I want you to always remember what I taught you when you wanted to give up and go in the house and watch TV, you cannot do anything sitting on your buttocks; it's all or nothing." Of course, he did not quite say it that nicely, but I knew exactly what he was talking about.

During my last visit to Centerville before my father passed, I spent a week with him when he was in the hospital. Little did

I know he had been in the hospital for a while before family members blew my phone off the hook asking me when I was coming to see him. I was confused why they were in such a rush for me to come to town, but that is when I found out he had been in the hospital for 10 days and was not sure if he would make it home. I was beyond upset, but I maintained my posture.

When I walked into the hospital room, he was fast asleep, but when he finally woke up, he looked straight at me and smiled real big and said, "You made it." He looked around and when it was just me and him in the room together, he whispered and said, "I am not sure if I will live much longer. All or nothing." As he was transported to another hospital, he grabbed my hand and said again, "All or nothing."

That week was a roller coaster ride! A week of unnecessary foolishness of people bickering over nothing. I prayed for wisdom and understanding. I needed God! I would sit there and stare at him in his humble state and think to myself, "Where was this father when I needed him the most?"

As I at his coffin, I wondered what was next. This man looked just like me, or I looked just like him. I knew that going through things strengthened you. I understood that your tears would one day turn into laughter. I got that the pain you faced today, would be your teacher or guide tomorrow. I could even hear the church mother and father saying, "Just hold on, weeping may endure just for one night, but joy will come in the morning." Yes, I truly understand that. I got it! But the pain, NOW, seems unbearable, unreal, WHY?

My life was a revolving door that I continued to go in and out. I was able to walk out of the shadow, but before I knew it, I found myself right back being who others wanted me to be and not who God would have me to be—another familiar shadow. I often found myself seen and not heard, or heard and not seen. God was pushing me forward, away from people, and into His arms.

Even though my father and I did not have the best relationship, I tried so hard to make him proud of who I had become. Anything I did or accomplished was never good enough for him. The only time I heard of how proud he may have been is when he was talking to others, but when speaking to me, all he would say was "you could do better." He always questioned whether I was living my life or if I was living my life for others. Little did he know.

In my earlier stages of life, I was so determined not to be a victim of abuse I became the abuser. I refused to look weak like I thought my mother was, not realizing I was becoming the very person I despised and that was my father. The person I stared at in the mirror daily was a person I did not like. Without realizing it, I was acting just like him. I was full of anger. I was hurt and very bitter. I was in a battle with myself. And, now staring at him lying there motionless, I realized the shadow was fear of myself.

For a season, from the age of 14 to around 24, I lived everybody else's purpose in life except mine. I was paralyzed with fear and doubt. I allowed what others thought of me to hold me back. I was a frightened little girl and that followed me into my adulthood. Yes, I walked with authority. I looked accomplished. Even though I had been delivered from people, I was still afraid to launch into the deep. I prayed and asked God to show me myself. And in the middle of my father's funeral, I heard God speaking directly to me. I had always been awake, but I had just woken up to another level in my life! I needed to see God for myself. I needed a me moment! So, while everyone else was listening to the man of God giving encouraging words, God was revealing myself to me. As the choir sang, "Late in the midnight hour, God is gonna turn it around," my feet got light and all I could do was praise God from within.

It was not until my father got sick that he told me how proud he was of me. It was hard to believe what had happened, even when standing in front of my father's coffin. He looked just like me. I stared because I saw the younger version of my father lying in the coffin, still and helpless. All eyes were on me while I stood there looking at my father's mouth glued shut; he had a childlike facial expression as though he was getting ready to say something crazy.

I was not excited about my father's death. Not at all! But I heard God speak directly to me, "THROUGH DEATH COMES LIFE!" Thank you, Jesus! God used this situation as a missing piece to the puzzle. In school I learned a shadow is an image where light from a light source is blocked by an object. The silhouette, better known as a shadow, becomes a reflection of the object the light is projecting against, which is usually two times the size of the actual object. All this time I had allowed my fear to paint a false reality of what was not there.

About the Author

Larvetricus R. Harris was born and raised in Clarksville, Tennessee on August 12, 1977. She is the oldest of two, born of Clement D. Moore (late) and Phala M. Hughes. She received most of her grade school education through the Clarksville school system and eventually graduated from Montgomery Central High School in 1996. On June 19, 2017, Larvetricus received an Associate of Art Degree in Business Administration from Strayer University. She is in the process of furthering her education to obtain a Bachelor of Arts degree in the same major. Not only being a speaker affiliated with faith-based organizations, Larvetricus has obtained Competent Communicator (CTM) in Toastmaster's International. Toastmaster's is an accredited international speaker's program.

Larvetricus is married to Nathaniel K. Harris. They have been married for fourteen years. Together, they have four (4) children: Ashley, Nathaniel Jr., Isaiah & Emmanuel Harris. Larvetricus and her husband, Nathaniel serve in many capacities as a team, along with coaching in a local sports program in Baltimore County, and serve as youth mentors.

Larvetricus serves as an Associate Pastor of L.I.F.E. Church Ministries, under the direct leadership of Senior Pastor Amin

T. Flowers. Through ministry and coaching, she has been preaching, teaching, and mentoring since she was 14 years of age and preached her 1st initial sermon on her 18th birthday in 1996. As an Evangelist, she traveled throughout the United States ministering to youth and adults alike. She has headed several youth groups, mentorship programs, daycares, after-school programs, revivals, and has served faithfully on many auxiliaries within the church.

Her favorite scripture is 2 Corinthians 4:8-9 KJV, "We are troubled on every side, yet not distressed; perplexed, but not in despair; persecuted, but not forsaken; cast down, but not destroyed."

www.ingramcontent.com/pod-product-compliance
Lightning Source LLC
Chambersburg PA
CBHW071743040426
42446CB00012B/2460